AF229551

For the Hurting Heart

A Collection of Poetry and My Journey Thus Far

"To everything there is a season, and a time to every purpose under the heaven.." Ecc 3:1 KJV

MISS JERRY LEE SCHOCK

A Loved One Has Crossed Over

They knew the time would come, when
they would have to say goodbye,
And their hearts are truly broken, as
for their loved one they cry.
But Lord we know that life and death
are truly in Your Hands,
And You have this sweet girl with You,
that was Your Master plan.

Their lives will seem so empty as
they journey on their way,
But peace and strength will come from
You, with each new passing day.
The memories they all will have of
times that now are passed,
Will bring a smile as they think of her
and times they shared will last.
She is in Heaven now, and Jesus
was waiting for her there,

As He guided her safely over, to
her Heavenly home so fair.
No more suffering, and no more
pain, will she ever feel again,
And someday soon we'll meet her,
waiting for us, with Him.

Given to me by the Lord
05/09/2016

As They Wait

As they wait -watching their loved
one-helpless are they all-
Praying for Your touch-as on Your Name they call-
Oh Father wrap each one close in Your arms of love-
As they wait and wonder when
she'll go to Heav'n above.
There is nothing we can do but
pray for strength and peace-
Until at last at home with You- she finds sweet relief.

For Miss Bertha 's family
02/25/07

He is Home

What can we say Lord? We knew
the day would come,
When suffering would end and
You would call him home.
It was never in our minds that he would leave so fast-
And yet in the midst of the pain,
we know he's home at last.

We say he was much too young
and this should never be-
But our lives are in Your hands-
the future we cannot see.
If we were to see trouble ahead
then we would often fret-
In facing the unknown with You as
guide-every need is met.

Angels surround each of us-when
You call a loved one home-
And You give us peace and comfort
to know we're not alone.
You've guided many a loved
one –safe to the other shore;
And we know one day we'll be there-with You
forevermore.

In Loving memory of
Wayne Sweat
8/16/08

Heaven is Sweeter

Heaven sure is sweeter, our brother made it home,
Thank You precious Father, he did not go on alone.
The angels stood by his bed
waiting, until it was time-
As Jesus stepped out and
said –he's here, he's mine.

He served You with a passion not many have today.
He knew when sickness came
and death was on the way-
That all was in Your hands and
You were by his side-
He started looking for Jesus
knowing in You he'd abide.

The grace that You have given
was present from the start-
And he knew that he was safe
with Jesus in his heart.
He sang nothing but praises for
You until the very end-
And when he crossed the river –he
found his dearest friend.

In Loving memory of
Wayne Sweat
8/3/08

Her Pain

Dear Lord, if I could have only one thing today,
It would be from my sister, the pain-You'd take away.
She seems to have more valleys,
than anyone I've known-
Yet my precious Father- through
each one she has grown.

You see- she is so very special -
to those of us who look,
Upon the very heart of her - that
reads like a precious book.
Her love for You is so like a perfume
that is fine and rare,
And I ask today dear Father, You
would grant this prayer.

As she lives her life for You - upon this earth below,
Please send her heavenly angels -to
set her face aglow
And let her feel a hug - that only You can give
From the One who'll walk beside her -
every day she'll live.

With love, from the Lord to Bertha

10/98

His Journey

He spent so many years driving up and down the road-
Carrying a burden for the lost-tho'not a part of his load.
He'd share his Jesus willingly with everyone he'd meet-
Whether on the road-or walking down the street-

He always came to church and
spent much time in prayer-
Grateful each and every time-
someone brought him there-
He praised the Lord for goodness
and grace beyond compare-
Even in the pain-you'd still find him sitting in that chair-

He's been ready to go home for such a long, long time-
And openly let those near him know,
for Heaven he did pine.
Today his journey is over –and
pain's a thing of the past-
He went to meet his Savior-and is now at rest at last.
God gave us many precious years
and memories are sweet-
Wait by the gate my brother-for
someday soon we'll meet.

In loving memory of Bro. Strange
04/02/07

I Am Waiting

Don't weep for me, children of mine-
don't be sad today.
I'm at rest now with my Lord-
safe in His arms to stay.
Part of me did not want to go-
as you waited through the storm,
But my trip became so easy
when the angels took me home.

I'm waiting now on Heavens shore
and in just a little while-
I'll meet you there with loved ones,
you'll know the reason I smile.
I served Him such a long time,
His Word I hid in my heart-
But I knew the day would come
when we would have to part.

I saw those eyes of love,
as I stepped on Heaven's shore
And knew I was free from the
pains of life forevermore.
Even though God let me suffer
He brought me through the pain-
As I desired others to see Him,
and peace and comfort to gain.

Remember when you think of me,
I don't want you to be sad-
But think I've just gone home-
and I'm waiting for you with dad.

Given to me by the Lord for Ellen and her family
As Miss Johnnie waits for us
7/22/2000

He's given us many comforts; He
has the right to take away.
To the Lord be praise and glory;
Now and ever, let us pray.

I Have Watched

I've watched as Satan's fought
you time and time again;
Yet I've seen you turn your eyes
to Heaven, and to Him.
I've watched as things have happened
that would surely break apart,
The love of many a Christian and
yet you've set your heart.

You've turned your eyes to Jesus;
you've given Him the praise,
You've suffered many, many things
in these past few days.
And yet the Lord has strengthened,
and brought you closer still.
Oh Lord, build a hedge of thorns,
as You do Your precious will.

I ask that You would take each one
and draw them close to You,
Soothe the pain they're feeling now,
do what only You can do.
Father You've given me a special
love for every one of them,
Jerry and Jeremy and Lisa and precious little Robin.

My precious Heavenly Father, may
Your perfect will be done,
But Lord I know their hearts are
broken, each and every one.
I ask you now to mend them, quickly, as days go by,
I ask that You will comfort them, for
Lord, we can't know why.

I pray that You will give a peace as only You can do
As the hedge of thorns grows higher,
from Heaven and You.
I pray You will protect them, wrap
them in Your arms of love
Send those guardian angels,
very quickly from above.

Given to me by the Lord 9/7/1996

In Loving Memory of Morris Lamb

He was a brother and a friend,
with a heart of purest gold,
How many people he cared for-
can never here be told.
He touched so many lives for the
short time he spent on earth-
Just taking care of others –he could
never have known his worth.

He was a tenderhearted man –by
his looks you could not tell-
But as he spent time doing for others-
his spirit would never fail.
Always doing his very best –even
putting his own needs aside-
He did all he undertook so well –and
in his work took pride.

He'd say "I'm here to take care of you guys
and Mike" and did the job so well.
To imagine not seeing him again in this
life-is the hardest thing to tell.
A friend in time of trouble who was
always there when you'd call,
Who never was too busy –even
when the orders were tall.

He could look at a project and imagine
an unseen beauty there -
And build anything without a plan –and
made it with such care.
He was at ease with his music, as
the guitar he would play-
And just as much at home in a boat-
fishing, the very next day.

He had an unseen talent hidden
well behind that smile -
Who would have known –he'd be
gone in such a short while?
He spent his last hours in a place he loved to be-
In the ocean, on a boat, watching the fish at sea.

To say that we will miss him is an
understatement it's true.
Just wish we could tell him one more time
"Morris, we love you".

Given to me by the Lord 10/3/2015
Gal 6:2

Mothers

Mothers are God's gift to enrich our
lives and help us as we grow,
The pain of losing our special friend
is much harder than we know.
They're our help in times of trouble
and encourage us on the way.
They teach us all about the Lord and
from them we learn to pray.

A mother shows us by her faith, what
a godly woman should be,
They love us through child hood, when
we're grown they set us free.
We'll miss Granny's quiet spirit and
seeing that precious smile,
As she sat and listened to the man
of God, preaching for a while.

We'll miss her tender -hearted ways
and just knowing she was here,
In the midst of all the hurt and pain,
will bring us peace and cheer.
The seat beside you may be empty
and although it will be strange,
In time you'll find the peace, that our
loss is truly Heaven's gain.

She has hurt so much in recent days
and now she'll suffer no more,
As she walks the streets of Heaven
with those who've gone before.
Granny must have watched from up above
and I'm sure she smiled again,
Knowing that even in the midst of
death - others were led to Him.

What a precious memory the Lord has
given to those she left behind,
We praise our Heavenly Father,
who even in death is so kind.
So hold on my precious sister and
rest in Jesus' arms for a while,
Until you're able to walk on your
own, and really want to smile.

Our prayers will bring you comfort as
the angels surround you today,
And bear you up in arms of love,
as you journey on your way.
Remember in the darkest of nights,
when the pain is hard to bear,
God touches an intercessor —to
hold you up in prayer.

Given to me by the Lord 2/21/10

My Heart Cries Out

Oh how my heart cries out for you -
as I petition God above,
To fill your life with peace, and
surround you with His love.
I know behind the smile- there you hide the tears,
And the pain I've seen you suffer
through - these past few years.

Yes, time will bring relief-as it has healed before,
And God will ease the pain, and
bring you peace once more.
But oh my precious sister, what a testimony I see!!!
As you walk through each valley -and
send to Him your plea.

You still can laugh and sing, and
praise the Father above,
You will never ever know how much,
you manifest His love.

Written in loving memory of Faye

One Day

One day in Heaven our Father
looked to the earth below;
And told another child to make the crossing I know.
His soft voice spoke the words;
it's time to come on home.
But rest assured those left behind
will never be alone.

The Father sends His angels to
guide you on your path,
Until sweet peace will fill your soul-
and ease your mind at last.
There will always be an empty
place – deep within your heart-
But very soon you'll find – we'll never be apart.

10/26/2016

Our Hearts Are Broken

Although our hearts are broken
and we cannot understand-
We know our Father in Heaven
has a Master plan.
One of the hardest things we 'll
ever do is lay a child to rest-
Yet deep within our sorrow
we know we have been blessed.

Our hearts are crying out in pain
to our Father up above-
Surround this precious family
and let them feel Your love.
Heaven must have needed an angel
and Jesus called her home-
Now we're left to wonder how
we'll ever make it alone.

But Father You see much farther
than we can ever see-
So help us as we lean on You –
dear Father is our plea.

Given to me by the Lord
walk this road of pain –
with much prayer
April, 2004

Praise to the Lord

As we look at Your creation and
You draw us ever near,
Even in the face of death, there
is still no need to fear.
Your promise is to keep us, no
matter how dark the night,
And down in the lowest valley, we
know You are the light.

Lord you know our hearts are breaking
for a loved one in pain,
You may even hear us question
You, what is there to gain?
But You can see much farther than we will ever see,
You plan each step along the
way —help us Lord we plea.

If we can praise You today-even
in the midst of the storm,
Soon we'll find that comfort and safety from all harm.

For Wayne and the family
as we wait on the Lord,
From the Lord with love
8/2/08

She's Gone on to Glory

She's gone on to glory and we are left alone-
But part of us is still at peace knowing she's at home.
Far from all she suffered, and far
from sickness and pain;
It truly is our loss but-
most surely Heaven's gain.

I hear her sweet voice singing I
can see the lights of home-
And close my eyes and envision
our Father on the throne.
Today she sees things clearer than
she's ever seen before-
For today she closed her eyes here
and woke on Heaven's shore.

For Miss Bertha 's family
02/26/07

The Burden

The burden is too great my Lord-no
daylight I can see –
The valley is too deep – please
come and rescue me!!
Each time my heart cries out – faithful
You've always been- Dear Father
here I am –praying once again.

I do not understand why others suffer so-
It may be precious Father -I'm
not supposed to know-
For each time You bring a burden –or
someone suffers pain;
It draws me to reach out to them –
in prayer once again.

You've touched my heart so many
times, I felt that it would break
As other's burdens I've tried to
bear –and intercession make.
Another precious one is hurting in their heart-
As one they held so dear –from this earth did part.

Strengthen them dear Lord, as only You can do,
Surround them now with angels
and draw them close to You.
Let them know the burden is carried to Your throne,
By many who love them –don't let them feel alone.

11-20-99

The Intercessor

Making sweet intercession-for all needs
great and small.
Trusting in God's wisdom-as on His
Name we call.
Lean not to thine own understanding –
trust only in the Lord-
And He will prepare all hearts,
according to His Word.

Standing in the gap we ask the Father
to meet your every need
To send wisdom and protection
from above
–as we pray and plead.

Given to me by the Lord
Proverbs 3:5 9/16/06

To Comfort You In Sorrow

When a loved one leaves this earth And
we're feeling all alone- Walking down a
dreary path, So dark and yet unknown.
The road ahead may not be easy-
Rocky places many it's true-
But I'm trusting He'll place angels-
On every side of you.

The pain you feel He surely knows
And understands today.
But He will help you bear the load-
He's allowed to come your way.
Comfort and peace may seem far-
But His promises are there.
He'll never leave or forsake us-
And He does truly care.

Given to me by the Lord
2-2-97

As We Wait

He's on his way to
Heaven as they wait
beside his bed-
Never did we
think of this, but by Your Hand we're led.
We do not want to see him suffer
or be in terrible pain,
But Father we seek Your will and
ask Your glory to gain.

His life reflects all Your goodness
and his legacy is grace.
With the death angel ever near-he
longs to see Your face.
We pray for peace and protection
for all that we hold dear-
And ask You bring them comfort
and wash away the fear.

We praise You for Your goodness
and for mercy and grace,
As we follow where You lead, and
seek that special place.

8/2/08

Dear Lord,

Our lives are changed forever, we will never again be the same. Our hearts are saddened at the home-going of our brother, Wayne, and yet we rejoice. I thank you Father that even the day we got the news he had cancer and the doctors said there was nothing that could be done, even then Lord there was a peace. Maybe because Wayne was at peace that You know best.

There is a terrible ache inside each of us and a hole in our hearts that nothing can ever fill. But You, Father, have the special touch we all need. I pray for that special healing touch when the hurt is so deep that even the tears will not come.

Our lives will be empty to a large extent-but they are so full and rich, just because you gave him to us for a while. Wayne was such a loving servant and sold out to You. He taught Your word in Sunday School with a passion. He spent many hours in preparation to feed us, his class. We are forever grateful that you allowed us to sit under his teaching as the Holy Spirit led him. He will never be replaced in the choir, or in the trio or playing for the services and many of us as we sang. Others may come join us, but there will never be another Wayne.

He is gone from our sight but never from our hearts. The love and memories that we have made with him-are ours forever. His home will never be the same, for he will not be there in the flesh. But it will be richer because he has been, just as the Choir and the trio and the entire church will be. His precious Sharon and all of the children and grandchildren and Miss Louise, his family, his precious brother Bill and sister Tina, will never be the same. Cindy will never be the same, none of us will. But they are also richer, because he was there to love and share their lives.

What will we do Lord? Wayne was such a part of us for so long and we will miss his presence and I will miss the special moments we shared as he asked me to pray for his precious family and friends as needs arose, or for a special need on his heart. I thank you the last words we ever spoke on this earth were sweet. I am sure he said a lot of "I love you's" the last day he was at church and heard the same. Those memories and special words will last forever.

As long as we have breath and life-Wayne will never be far from us. He will remain in our hearts and very much a part of our daily lives. Even though he rests with you as we wait for Your return-we know that he is happy and at peace-so we can take solace in Your goodness and grace. But we still feel the loss that Heaven gained. Thank You for letting each of us have this sweet man and friend in our lives for such a short time. Thank You for loving us so much and for all the joy and sweetness You spread over us as we try to serve You and others.

Just Your daughter,

Jerry

What A Precious Angel

What a precious angel You sent to bless us Lord-
As Bertha sang and praised You
in song, and thru the Word-
Her voice is stilled on earth but
in Heaven she still sings
You took our precious loved one-
home on angel wings.

She wanted to be with you-but
she still wanted to stay-
Please don't let her suffer Lord-we all came to pray.
She spent some time here- with
Your angels in her room-
They brought to her Your promises that death
need not mean gloom.

She lingered between life and
making her journey home-
But in Your grace and goodness –
she left us all alone.

In loving memory of Miss Bertha,
03/18/07

With Deepest Sympathy

No one can really understand or
know the pain you feel,
But the Lord above in Heaven, who can, and
surely will. Sometimes in this life there are
valleys we must go through, But I know our
Lord and Savior, is watching over you.

In His word He gives the promise,
of angels to protect,
And the Holy Spirit to guide us,
we know He won't forget.
The pain that is inside you, the world may never see,
It hides behind the smile you wear,
but cannot be hidden from me.

My heartfelt prayers go out to you, as
another cross you bear, And I pray that it
will help you, to know how much I care.
There are no words in this world,
to bring you comfort now;
But I pray that guardian angels
will hover near somehow.

And spread their wings around
you, until your pain is past;
And give you blessed peace and consolation at last.

Psalm 91:1,2,4,11,12

With Heartfelt Sympathy

There is little that anyone can do
and less that one can say
But ask the Lord to comfort you as
you walk this road today.
No one can really understand the
pain that you will bear,
But I pray somehow it comforts you
to know that other's care.

And knowing in those tear filled
days that you still must face,
Our Father up in Heaven, will send
an extra measure of grace.
Without your precious loved one to
help you through the day,
The Lord will send His angels to
guard you on the way.

In His words He gives the promise
of angels to protect,
And the Holy Spirit to guide us,
we know, He won't forget.
Know that many prayers will be
sent to the Father above,
Asking Him to send His angels and
surround you with His love.

Psalm 91:1,2,4,11,12
Given me by the Lord,
September 7, 1996

Her Light Still Shines

Miss Nellie's gone to Heaven, and
life will never be the same,
Yet Lord we're so much richer for
the lessons we have gained.
She taught her children well, and
loved her husband true,
But the center of all she did, our
precious Lord was You.

Every time the choir sang, "I Was
Born to Serve the Lord",
Miss Nellie's image was in our
minds —of her reading the Word.
She was such a precious angel , as
beside her husband she'd walk;
And in each conversation was praise
for You , every time she'd talk..

The light that shown around her daily
came from very deep within-
Now that light shines bright in Heaven —but
on earth it will never dim.
The legacy she leaves behind is
one of truth and Jesus' love-
A message that is never-ending-
sent from Heaven above.

Lord You know we are so grateful
for the little time we had;
But we are sure -You understand-
within our hearts we are sad.
Her voice is stilled upon the earth
but in Heaven it clearly rings-
Her praises for You will never end —as
with Your choir she sings.

For Miss Nellie's family
—as we mourn our loss, and celebrate Heaven's gain.
12/25/10

In Loving Memory of Theresa Buechler

Dear Lord You know we'll miss her
and her precious smiling face,
She surely was our special angel-
overflowing with grace.
The smallest gift would bring a smile
and fill her with such cheer,
And then you could see that grin-
spreading from ear to ear

Even in the midst of pain she had in times gone past-
She'd praise Your precious Name-
and say it will not last.
She had a great sense of humor and
laughter came easy to her.
She loved the Lord and people-
that you knew for sure.

When she graduated to Heaven
with Jesus holding her hand,
The faith she had became sight –there in glory land.
The pain is gone and the smile wide,
as she greets loved ones there-
Praising the Lord for all He's done
and His tender, loving care.

Even though we miss her and our
hearts are filled with pain-
In just a little while we know, we all will meet again.

In loving memory of Theresa Buechler
Psalm 116:15
Given to me by the Lord
2/29/2012

Balm Of Protection

Today there's a balm of protection
easing some of the pain-
We know that earth's loss,
is surely Heavens gain.
Tomorrow and in days ahead
the reality will be known,
Mama's no longer with us and
yet we're not alone.

Though we can't reach out and touch
the one we've loved for many years
We'll remember all her love and
smile through the tears.
Our hearts are saddened-but
For us you see
For in Heaven there is now
A jubilee.

With love,
Miss Jerry

Dear Lord,

We wait and we wonder, but God, You already know the answer. Our thoughts of the unknown overtake our mind at times, and we fret, and ask, what if? But You have promised to meet our every need. And Lord, my sister and her husband and children are in need of peace. If there are words I am to give them, they will only come from you. My heart aches as I bring the need to You daily. I have seen many things come along and have spent hours praying and seeking Your face to have their needs met, and You have always been faithful. This is beyond our control as so many things have been, but nothing in the life of a Christian is out of Your control. I confess as we face the unknown, our faith sometimes will falter. But Lord, You suddenly renew it by giving us those blessings when we least expect them. The valley ahead may be rough and it may seem un-ending at times, but we can rest assured You have already walked the road ahead of us. Every step we will take with her, has already been taken by You, as You go ahead and prepare the way. Help us as we walk through this unknown time with her, to remember that You are in control. We may never know on this earth, the why of what lies ahead, but we know the way, because You lead us. At times our feet may stumble, but You will never let us fall. At times the way may be rocky and the clouds may hide the sun from us, but it surely will shine again. The valley will become a mountaintop before we realize it, and we will look down and know in our hearts that You led us all the way. You carried us when we could not walk, You held us in your arms when the pressure of it all closed in on us, and You held tight to our hand as our feet touched the rocky places. You will dry every tear we will or have already shed, facing the unknown. We take peace in the knowledge that You are in control and You never have or never will make a mistake, as we face life and the challenges it gives us. We already know in our hearts, that nothing ever touches the child of God, but what it has already been approved at the throne of grace. We have spent many long hours in prayer as we seek Your will. Father, we already know that where You guide, You provide. Give each of us around our sister and her family, the wisdom to hear what You want them to have from each of us. Whatever the outcome, You will be there with us and things always look better from Heaven's point of view. Help us to cling to each other, to You and to Your promises from your Word, as we wait and we wonder, and pray, to know that You have it all under control.

Just Your daughter,

Jerry

Gal. 6:2

Home Before Nightfall

You prayed I'd go before night fell,
and all memory was gone-
The Father answered your prayers,
because I could not go on.
My body had grown so weary and
my mind was growing dim,
So my Savior came to get me –and
take me home with Him.

Right now there is such a sadness,
you think will never end,
But you'll have the sweetest
memories fill your heart again.
The Savior has promised faithfully-
you will never be alone-

Remember those promises daily,
you are not on Your own.

My presence will hover nearby-in everything you do,
I know the valley is not forever,
and Jesus is holding you.

For Miss Nellie's Family
From the Lord 12/28/10

How Deep the Valley?

The valley seems so deep Lord, will it ever end?
Yes my precious child, you will feel whole again.
I know the pain you feel and see the tears you cry,
But my promises are true, each teardrop I will dry.

I'm with you in the valley –you are not on your own-
For in My Word I've promised, you'll never be alone.
I'll carry you through this valley as I have in the past,
When we're through the valley,
peace will come at last.

I never promised roses or a life without any pain,
But in the end, My child, you'll be the one to gain.
Your Mama's safe in Heaven and
waiting here for you,
Along with many loved ones, who are waiting too.

Given to me by the Lord for the Moore Family
12/27/10

I can hear Miss Nellie-say from
up on Heavens shore:
Don't weep my precious loved
ones-I am safe forevermore.
My love for you will never die,
you will never be alone.
Remember lessons I taught you-
while you were at home-

Remember to love each other-and
stay very close to the Lord;
Walk the straight and narrow way,
depending on His Word.
Remember all the good times and
the fun we always had,
Be sure to look after each other, especially your Dad.

He took good care of us and
preached the Word so true,
Now He needs extra comfort, that
can only come from you.
Be true to all I taught you and
share freely of your love,
And very soon I'll meet you all in Heaven up above.

Given to me by the Lord for the Moore Family
12/27/10

I've Watched You

I've watched you - oh so many times,
with a smile upon your face,
Hiding tears and pain inside -
covered only by His grace.
The pain you hide so well within, as
you see a loved one leave,
May be hidden from the world -
but I still see the grief.

So I ask the Father draw you close
to Him -with comfort all around
Wrap you in His arms of love - and
with angels -you - surround.
Another now is free from pain -and
finally she's at rest,
I can almost see the Father - draw
her close to His breast-

And hear Him welcome her to Heaven -and
the joy bells as they ring-
Hush!! I hear a heavenly choir - can
you hear her as she sings?
With trouble gone - the tears are
dried-no more will she feel pain-
This earthly vessel of clay gone
home -will never hurt again.

She's waited- like us- for the promise-of
a meeting on that shore-
Where, when we get to Heaven -
there's parting, nevermore.

For Miss Bertha
- In loving memory of Faye
10/26/2016

Life With My Sisters

Life brings unexpected blessings,
as we travel on our way.
Mine has been my Sisters, each and Every day.
We've shared both pain and sorrow,
And laughs along the way.
Ollie and Linda, Lessie and Jane.

We shared the happy times and even bore the pain.
We have depended fully on the Lord.
And trusted in His Word.
Through good times and through bad,
Always we did gain.

There is No way to say-How Special you are to me.
And Daily as I pray-for Him to meet the needs.
I ask Him to protect you all
As on His name you call.

I love you ALL,
More than you can EVER know.
Your Sister,
Ecc 3:1

Dear Father,

I am at a loss for words. Cindy and I talked about this time, she dreaded it so much, and yet it is real. Our precious Miss Nellie is now in Heaven. Lord I know You were there to take her hand when she made that crossing. You answered so many prayers. You took her before night fell. I so well remember asking on the way to work before she went into surgery, Lord if You are going to take her home, please don't take her from the operating table, and You did not. You waited and gave her family a chance to hold her hand and be with her before You came for Your precious angel.

Never has there been another precious gem like Miss Nellie. She is one of a kind. I can still hear her asking June who she was talking to when calling to check on Preacher Moore-and when June told her Miss Jerry she said I want to talk to her- much to our surprise. She told how the girls had decorated her house and how pretty it looked and when I ask if they were taking good care of her she said they always did. She let me know she was watching Cindy so she wouldn't get rid of her clothes, what a beautiful breath of fresh air!! I told her I was still praying for her every day and just like always she replied "well don't stop" and I promised not to and said I love you Miss Nellie and she said I love you. Never did I dream that would be our last conversation. Once again Lord -how grateful- Mother raised us saying if we had anything to say to someone or do for them, to do it now because we may never have another opportunity. Thank You Lord-those are the last words we said. I love you-3 small words that carry so much power. I love You Lord and am so grateful You love me even though this finite mind will never understand how –we know You love all Your sinful children.

Thank You for so many sweet memories in the 18 ½ years we knew each other. How pleased she was over the new furniture for the parsonage on Holcomb Bridge-she could not get over it-thanks for letting me be involved in that selection. How excited she was to show us through the home she grew up in when they moved, sweet times. She would get so excited over the smallest things. A poem or a few words of encouragement You would give me for her brought the biggest smile. And always-that special hug we would get and the "I love you" we always said- and then she would plant a kiss on my cheek. Precious memories Lord only You can give.

How wonderful that her girls got to spend some quality time with her this past month. It will not take the sting away of her not being with them but let them draw on those times when the going gets rough. When it gets hard Lord –for each of them-I pray You would flood them with her love and Your peace. She is the perfect example of a Christian, a woman, a mother, a wife and friend. Our loss is Heaven's gain. And what a loss we feel. It will never be the same for any of us who were blessed to be around her or sing with her or cook beside her as we did so many times at the old Galilean. Just being around her was refreshing.

Surround Preacher Moore with comfort and peace, his loss is so great because he loved her so many years. His whole life he looked after her and faith pulled them through many things he shared with us, and just as many he did not. Pour that faith and all Your promises over her family like sweet honey. Bear the hurt for them Lord-let our prayers take away the sting and pain.

All too soon we will say farewell to her and honor her for the last time over here-but we are all grateful we will see her again, over there. What a blessed hope and thought. I imagine Miss Bertha, Wayne, Martha, Jim, Bro Paul and many others waited for her crossing and greeted her. Now they are all spending Christmas with Jesus this year!! As Bro. Rex said, Miss Nellie made it home before Christmas. We are happy for her and sad for us, but we know she will never again forget where her purse is or that she has grandchildren or where she left something or not know a loved one standing in front of her. She will never feel another pain or shed another tear over a wayward child. Thank you for that Lord, thank You for Miss Nellie. All our lives are so much richer because she was a part of them. We all love her so much and her precious family. Thank You Lord for bringing me to Galilean 18 ½ years ago and for letting me share the trials and triumphs we have had and will have. We love You and trust You to handle it all, because You are our Father.

Just Your daughter,

Jerry

Our Mother's

Our Mother's are so special to
us- each and every day,
And our hearts can feel so broken
when they are called away.
Heaven surely needed another rose –to
brighten the garden there.
So the Father called her home –to
a place with no more care.

And someday we'll make the crossing –and
find her on that shore-
And we will praise the Lord together –and
shed our tears no more.

–With much love and Prayer
in the homegoing of your Mother-
4/13/08

She went to sleep on earth last night,
but in Heaven she awoke;
Even though you will miss her –
even though your hearts are broke,
You know with the Heavenly choir –
today your sister will sing;
Throughout the streets of Heaven –
her angel voice will ring.
The Father's made a promise,
one day we'll meet again,
The time we all look forward to –
though we cannot know just when.

I've watched as time and again
you've seen a loved one go home,
Depending on God for all the peace-
you'd never find alone.
I am grateful for His love,
that truly will sustain,
All whom she will leave –
those who must remain.

By Jerry L. Schock
10-6-98

Someday there will no tears fall from our
eyes- No pain will break our hearts
When we meet our blessed Savior in the skies-
Where from loved ones, we'll never part.

The place your loved one moved to, is
still to us unknown, But surely he was
ready, his body, weary had grown.
One day we'll cross the river – into a land
that now seems far- And know the truth he
now sees, as we join the brightest Star.

One day in Heaven our Father looked
to the earth below; And told another
child to make the crossing I know.
His soft voice spoke the words,
it's time to come on home.
But rest assured those left behind will
never be alone. The Father sends His
angels to guide you on your path,

Until sweet peace will fill your soul-and ease
your mind at last. There will always be an
empty place – deep within your heart-
But very soon you'll find – we'll never be apart.

For Bill Sweat in the homegoing
of his father 3/10/97

The Garden

There is a garden up in Heaven,
With a gate we cannot pass through,
Until the time arrives, Jesus calls for me and you.
Our loved one has gone on, and we feel so alone;
But the Heavenly Father never leaves
us on our own. His love surely will
sustain us in painful days to come,

He bears the burden with us-one day
we will go home. Forever we'll be united
with those we hold so dear;
Until then the Father is waiting to dry our every
tear. May His love sustain and keep you until again,
we meet; As I pray for peace and comfort –
kneeling at Jesus feet.

The Homegoing

Another beautiful angel, just entered Heavens gate.
But Lord, we miss her so, why could You not wait?
She's mine now, My dear child,
I needed her with Me.
Her body no longer suffers, I set her spirit free.

She brought you joy for just a
while-I left her there 'tis true.
I had to let you see just how
much I really do love you.
I know your heart is broken and
the pain it goes so deep-
But this was my own special rose,
I could not let you keep.

She was sent to brighten up your world, so
often filled with care; Now she rests within
My arms, as you and I, the pain will share.
I'll carry you My child, until the peace will come,
You never will forget her, then one
day I'll call you home-

Tears will become a memory, as will the
pain you feel today- But remember I have
promised I will be with you always.

Psalm 34:18 91:11,12

The Long Road

It's been such a long road, full of so much pain,
And yet I know my sister has only Heaven to gain.
She'll win the battle she has fought,
no matter how it ends,
Should You decide to heal her,
or life come to an end.

Her faith is like a candle, lighting all she's near-
Her voice is filled with calmness-never doubt or fear.
Her life has been a light for all the world to see-
No matter what the path it took-she saw the victory.

She's prayed so many times for You to heal her Lord,
So she might continue on,
spreading Your Holy word.
But Father, life is slipping oh too fast away-
And yet she's looking forward to a brighter day.

Wrap her in Your arms of love,
as she nears that shore-
Hold her close and comfort her-as
angel's guide her o'er.

Psalm 23 For Miss Johnnie
Given to me by the Lord 5/9/2000

The Loved One's He Has Taken

The loved one's He has taken, to glory up above;
Leave our lives so empty and longing for their love.
But we know beyond all doubt,
waiting on a distant shore,
That our precious loved one, will suffer nevermore.

You've seen your closest friends
and a son's precious wife,
Joining our Father in Heaven -called
away from this life.
And yet you stand before Him -though
wounded as a bird;
Singing His glory and praise, like I have never heard!

The hurt within your heart -is
hidden from many eyes;
But I can see it - yes my precious sister, I do realize.
It is at a time like this, when there
is nothing one can say;
All I can do for you is send many
prayers, Heaven's way.

I know that time will help heal,
some of the hurt and pain;
But only God in Heaven - sees
you suffer, time and again.
I'm asking for those angels- to
surround you with His love;
To guide each step you take -
from Heaven up above.

I ask for you protection - and a
peace beyond all measure;
For in you, I see my sister, a very special treasure.
Someday very soon-we'll join our loved one's there-
And thank the Father above-we'll never have a care,

The Pain, The Peace

Father, how we hurt inside, when a loved
one goes away, And we are left behind to
cope, with each new passing day.
Sometimes we cry and even smile,
remembering things they have done;
Inside our hearts they are alive, we
can't believe, they're gone.

Death is one thing in this life, where we have no control;
It is the time we wonder, will I ever again be whole?
Our spirits and our hearts, cry out to You in pain;
Oh please, my Heavenly Father, take away the rain.

Let me see the sun shine, for just a little while,
Send quickly to my face, the sweetness of a smile,
For the only victory I have found,
as I travel through this life,
Is the victory You have given, in the middle of my strife.

You know my heart is aching, You see the tears I shed,
You know that so very deep within, there
are things I dread. But today my Heavenly
Father, Your Presence will be so real,
As around my very being, Your own arms, I feel.

Yes today I will find comfort and peace will not escape;
Because You walk beside me, with every step I take.

Psalm 23
7-24-98

The Path

The path is rough and stony, I
cannot go on alone, I said.
Come on my precious child, there is
nothing to fear, for I have gone ahead.
But Lord, the way is strange to me,
I fear the dark, I dread,
Hold on my precious child, for by My
own hand, you will be led,

Oh Father, I feel so alone, without
my loved one near.
I know My precious child, but I
needed them to be here.
I feel the pain burning deep within, when
from loved ones you must part;

But 'til you can see the light ahead, I'll
hold you closer to My own heart.

Please trust in Me, My dear child,
I know what's best for you;
I see much farther down the road
than anyone it's true,
I know the questions in your mind
and know you wonder why.
But just stay close to Me, My child,
each teardrop I will dry.

Someday you will understand,
when life on earth will end;

Then in My presence you will find,
I am your dearest friend.

Given me to by the Lord 7/24/98

The Whisper of Her Wings

Such a gentle breeze is blowing,
across this place today-
It's the angel wings of your loved one-
who to Heaven flew away.
She's resting now with Jesus and is
waiting for you there- You have the sweet
assurance- she's forever in His care.

She's met the other loved ones
who've gone on before-
And has already made the crossing
where she'll live forevermore.
Rest now in the in the promise of
the Savior we hold dear-
Even though you miss her – there
is nothing you should fear.

Just as she crossed over on the
journey to Heaven above-
You'll someday make that crossing
to live forever in His love.

10-1-96

There's A Road Ahead

There's a road ahead
that's dreaded without the
one we love;
But soon we know
You'll take her, to live in Heaven above,
Our hearts are fearful dear Lord,
to think of life alone;
And now we must confess we fear what is unknown-

You've given her more time than
we ever thought You'd give
As we held her close in prayer and
love-just hoping she would live
But as time is growing shorter and
we know she is in pain
We have to ask You Father-what is there to gain?

But deep inside we know it's all within Your Hand
And tho' we can't comprehend-it is part of Your plan.

For Miss Bertha's family
From Miss Jerry
02/25/07

Today we said goodbye to a precious sister here-
And though our hearts are sad, and we shed a tear –
You've given us the promise we will meet again,
Lord, help us to remember that in the end, we win.
As she made her journey to
Heaven, in the angels care-
Jesus held her hand to usher her over there.

She is safe and free from pain, with her Savior now,
We will have the strength, to make
it through somehow.
Heaven really isn't far and the time is drawing near,
When we will leave this world and
our hearts will fill with cheer

Given to me by the Lord,
In loving memory of Miss Theresa
3/1/2012
Psalms 116:15
"Precious in the sight of the LORD is the death of his saints."

Father here I am again asking for peace and comfort, as those You have given me to care for through intercession, are hurting. I confess I hurt with them, but Lord, You taught me long ago not to question You. Time and time again You have shown me, we may not understand why things happen, but we never have to question Your wisdom. As we said goodbye -for a while- to Miss Theresa, my heart was saddened but so glad for her. She went to Heaven very quietly with You taking her across the river and the angels ushered her in through those gates with You holding her hand. Oh yes!! You promised NEVER to leave us and as I heard those precious words from the scripture again I knew You came for her-Precious in the sight of the Lord is the death of His saints!!! That is one journey we will not make alone.

My heart aches for Sarge and those left behind-but through experience-You have taught the hurt will not last forever. The sting is still fresh and the empty place in our hearts and lives is too strong right now to look at the blessings. And yet I must-Miss Theresa did not have to suffer as some have-in uncontrollable pain-she did not have to lay in bed for months unable to move or talk –she did not have to stay in a hospital but You let her stay home where she could be more comfortable and surrounded by love. You even allowed her to be in church and let us really enjoy her almost to the end– she had the sweetest spirit. She loved everyone and You were her first love.

She truly enjoyed praising You as the choir sang and the preacher preached. One lady told me as we called the church for her arrangements-that she enjoyed watching Miss Theresa clap her hands as the choir sang-a few weeks before You came for her. What a blessing she and Sarge have been to me. I can remember as we went down the road more than once to a singing –her putting me in the front seat so I wouldn't get sick-she always looked after me. For nearly 20 years we shared our Birthday. I remember she looked at the cubic zirconia studs in my ears one Sunday and raved about how pretty they were. I told her they were really not expensive but she liked them so much I had to get her a pair. She was like a kid when I handed that box to her and I can see her grin from ear to ear and reach up for those hugs and a sweet kiss on the cheek we always got every time we met. And how I told Sarge I would keep her right beside me at the ladies meeting so she would not wander off and I did. Gladys had a cough and Miss Theresa pulled out those special cough drops she used and insisted Gladys use them. She was so precious and always such a pleasure. She was very opinionated and not afraid to say so but never meanly, always in love. Linda said when they went to a Campmeeting she was at the door every morning making sure Linda was up and properly dressed. Sarge even told her to remember Linda was a big girl. And as the choir traveled so many years she and Sarge were right there rooting us on.

She will live forever Lord, because she will always be in our hearts and memories. Please comfort her family during these dark days. Surround each of them with angels, and when the grief overtakes them, as it does all of us, wrap them up in Your own arms and let them rest their heads against Your breast as You have done for me so many times. Surround them with angels of peace and comfort and let them know not one day goes by that an intercessor is not pleading for them. Let them feel Your warmth as the Son shines on them.

Thank You so much precious Father for always being there for us, for Your precious promises and the precious ones You allow us to meet along life's way. Most of all thank You for Your precious promises that guarantee us a place in Heaven to be reunited with those we love and especially with You.

Just Your daughter,

Jerry

My Journey Thus Far
Romans 8:28

God is allowing my story to be told in print with this book.

When Mom and Dad were first divorced my Grandma Herman told Mom she could not raise us alone. Grandma told her to put us in the children's home and Mom said no. She said she would raise us no matter how many jobs it took She always said she was not raising us alone-God was watching over us.

For a while we stayed with Grandma and Grandpa Herman. Since I was the first granddaughter and born on Grandpa's 77th birthday-he favored me. Every Saturday morning, he and I would walk down the back alley the several blocks to Andy's Market. I loved garlic bologna and he would buy me a ring of garlic bologna and get his block of limburger cheese. Mom loved that too, but I could never even taste it. On the way home we would stop at the Texaco station and he would get me a chocolate bar. We would sit at that big kitchen table he had built-being a carpenter by trade- and he would get the saltine crackers, cut up the bologna for me and then start on his cheese. Grandpa loved the Cincinnati Red's baseball team and we would watch it on TV-him in his easy chair-me at his feet and his parakeet, Petey on his head.

Mom would take us kids roller skating down the sidewalks in Miamisburg and when my Uncle would come home from Panama we had family get togethers in the back yard where we all 3 helped Grandma and Grandpa in the garden they kept. Good memories.

We later moved to Parkside homes and on Sunday- Mom would put my youngest brother in the stroller- Stan behind him -and I would hold onto the bar. We would walk across the grassy area to the Lutheran church for Sunday School. As we got older, we moved closer to downtown Dayton and the 3 of us would walk to the City Mission for Sunday School where Hobart and Thelma Roark handled services. They owned a fur shop and furniture store in Laura, OH., and went to Westwood Baptist Church.

Thelma took an interest in me and Mom would let her pick me up on Friday and stay with them until after church Sunday. Saturday we would go for a walk and back home to eat and clean up. Then to the furniture store where she played the piano or organ and I would sing. The manager, Dick Foreman taught me how to greet customers. My first exposure to what became my career, the furniture business.

Saved at age 13 at the Westwood Baptist Church in Dayton, I wanted to tell everyone how to get saved. Mom worked at the YMCA as a cashier in the cafeteria and had exchange students from the Dominican

Republic. I invited Ramon Diaz to church. Taking my first visitor to church felt good, UNTIL we got into the church. 63 years later I STILL remember the cold feeling going down that aisle -it was as if someone poured a tray of ice over the entire church! All because his skin was darker. After quite a while my Sunday School teacher took me home and told Mom to pull me out of the church because I was being persecuted as I thought everyone should be treated the same My heart was broken but I determined to become a Missionary nurse and go to Africa so I could spread the gospel.

We were raised to believe the color of one's skin had nothing to do with anything-we did not know the word prejudice. We all went to school together from grade school through high and wondered what the big deal was when in the early 60's the schools in Dayton were to be integrated-we had always been together. My best friend all the way through grade and high school was Virginia Glanton, a black girl. Mom said you could cut anyone and we ALL would bleed red. Mom had a Dayton Daily Newspaper branch as one of her 3 jobs and we had a bowling team and a baseball team. One Saturday morning Mom took us bowling for the news branch to a bowling alley on Brown Street. One of our carriers was Calvin Jones -a black boy-and the manager of the bowling alley pointed at him when we went in to get our shoes and said "he can't bowl here". But Mom said, "if he can't bowl then none of us will and NO ONE from the Dayton Daily News will ever bowl here again". Needless to say, we ALL bowled- and integrated that bowling alley then and there!

Even though I found another church it was not the same –I graduated from Stivers High School high school in 1961 -10th in a graduating class of 161. Two highlights in school were the lead part I had in "Oklahoma" and the Bible Club teacher asking me to speak. When asked what I wanted to speak on, I said faith and she wrote the word acrostically and it said Forsaking All I Take Him. I have never forgotten it.

I started nurses training at Miami Valley Hospital and during my first year-allowed a man 8 years older than myself to take advantage of me. Thank God He forgives our failures when we confess and ask. Although Doug did all he could to make me lose my baby he failed. He got married the day before we were to be. Unmarried and pregnant-I turned to my best friend-Mom. When I called and told her she just said, "you better pack your clothes and come home".

Bobby Joe was born November 14, 1962. We lived at home for a few years and then moved to West Carrollton, OH. with a friend who had a son the same age as Bobby. We eventually got our own apartment and I bought a car. When the job at Penker Construction ended, I went around the corner to Roberts furniture to apply for a job-where they sold everything for the home. Howard Smith gave me a customer to see what I could do and when I sold a pair of lamps, hired me at once-saying if I could sell accessories, I could sell anything. Worked there until the owner bankrupted the company and moved back to Kentucky. In 1971, Ken Fletcher, Howard Smith and Don Wright bought the bankrupt stock. Ken called and asked if I wanted to come back to work-said Smitty told him if they were to succeed -they needed me. Of course, I did!! We could not afford a new sign so changed the name from ROBERTS to ROBERDS -switching the T to a D and thus Roberds Furniture was started.

Over time we had a total of 28 stores/distribution centers in 4 states and except for two in GA -I was instrumental in opening all of them as corporate coordinator. I was in FL opening 2 new stores when Bobby Joe was killed in a motorcycle wreck May 21, 1986. Neighbors said the police had been to the house God let me buy in 1974, several times to let me know and when they could not reach me, called my brother Jerry-whom they knew was a Deputy for Montgomery County, and he called my boss. Ken Fletcher did not know the Lord as far as I know but I prayed daily for him. He did not want me to talk about the Lord at work. Still He had my preacher come to the store to call me in FL to let me know. God had already arranged things as He always does.

Mom had retired at 65 on May 10th -her birthday- from the YMCA and Ken asked her at Bobby's funeral if she was going to move into my house-telling her I did not need it as I would be traveling. She said yes and Jerry moved her in June 1st. Mom lived there until she went home to be with the Lord July 19, 2011. After my move to GA the rent and payments were too much but both of my brothers offered to split the house payment and it was done 3 ways so Mom could stay where she was happiest. I appreciate them both and love them for their caring ways.

I had asked to move to FLORIDA in 1987 and continued to open stores between GA and FL and OH. June of 1992, Ken called saying we had stores in trouble in GA and he needed me to move there since I was the only one who could fix it. Serving and settled in my church-I told Ken I had to pray about it-I heard a gasp on the other end of the phone but that is all I can do when a decision is needed. He asked how long it would take to get an answer and I was confident God would let me know by Monday and told him so. He told me it would mean a $24000.00 salary and I had to be sure God was in the move not me. I prayed all weekend and only asked 2 things of the Lord so I would KNOW it was Him, not me. I said Lord please do not ever let me drive on 85 and not one dime will come out of my pocket to make the move (The company paid no expenses ahead of time). Monday, I called and asked the questions-they would get my apartment -pay first month's rent and deposit and all utility deposits would be made-close to the store. And, they would give me a check for the $3000.00 moving expense ahead of time. So, feeling confident it WAS God in charge-I said I would go-and he wanted me there in 3 weeks. I made some calls from the Shepherd's guide to see what churches were near Norcross and the first call was Galilean Baptist. 27 years later I am still there-God always knows where we belong, and I have never had to drive 85 or 285 to get to work. July 14, 1992, I moved my letter to Galilean and the 2nd week Ollie and Linda "adopted" me into their family. Linda's favorite saying is we are all kin under the skin. Even thought they never met Mom they loved her and she loved them.

With the move to GA I uncovered over $450,000.00 that had been stolen from the company and we moved the thieves out. Taking over inventory control helped and by December we had 21 people behind bars for theft.

We continued to open stores in all markets as I traveled from GEORGIA to FLORIDA to OHIO and opened one in INDIANA with my shock list rather than me as I was in GEOGIA solving issues. In 1996 we opened Roberds Grand in Cincinnati, OH. -a megastore-nearly 6 acres, larger than Riverfront Stadium.

I lived in the apartment until 1997 and signed the papers on my birthday to buy a condo-after the apartment owners wanted to raise the rent over $100.00 per month. I saw an ad for a realtor on TV and called Sherrell to ask where she went to church. She told me and asked why that question. I explained God knew where I needed to be but if she did not know Him, she could not listen to Him. It was clear God let me know I could spend $60,000.00 for a condo and she told me I would never find one for that. I explained she could not nor could I- but He knew where it was and 22 years later, I am still here (price was $59,900.00).

After opening a Distribution Center in GA-we moved our appliance and furniture Customer Service teams there. Every morning some of us would meet in my office and pray for one another and the business. June of 1999, our CFO from corporate called and Bob said he understood I was having prayer meetings in my office. I said yes, he told me he loved me and I know he did-but he could not allow me to continue, etc. I told him if he took God's hand off the business, we would lose it and he said he could not help it-Dec. that year the company filed a Chapter 13. By June, 2000, the liquidators were scheduled in and not wishing to watch nearly 30 years of my life's work torn apart-I took my 3 weeks vacation and resigned, without prospects. I went home and remember laying my keys on the coffee table and telling the Lord I NEVER wanted to be in the furniture business again. Three weeks later I was working for a computer company in Covington where one of my road techs had gone. By October it became evident there was something else awaiting and after praying about it I resigned.

Nov. 2000, a call came from one of young men that had been at Roberds and was now at the then Plan It Oak-we later named it Underpriced Furniture-asking if I was working-he said we have had the rest now want the best-they needed someone to run Customer Service. Nov 7th when I went to work there my entire work life changed for the better!! Thanksgiving meant the company provided meat and we all bought side dishes in for the meal. As we gathered in the break room at the warehouse-Mike Hall -the owner-asked if I would pray!! I was sure I had died and gone to Heaven!! In the nearly 18 years I worked -Mike and Tim encouraged me to pray-spread the gospel and lead our folks to the Lord. When Mike handed me my ring for 10 years of service-he kindly said, "If we have a spiritual leader-it is Jerry". I am truly blessed. Several young people will be in Heaven because of the freedom they gave me. I have thanked God many times for NOT listening to me. I finally retired Sept 2018.

One of most wonderful blessings going to work for Mike has been my "adopted" granddaughter Gladys Everson -she calls me Nana. Most of the kids at work still call me that as we keep in touch. I am ever so grateful we did not learn prejudice growing up or I would have missed this sweet girl and the sisters God gave me at church. One day when I arrived at the Distribution Center we had opened in 2007-there was a sign that said "No Parking Except for Nana"-Lauren, Mike's daughter had ordered from Amazon. They waited until just within the last couple of months to remove it.

All the wonderful names I have been called down thru the years and the sweet things that have been said are flooding my mind. I remember Mom saying if you have something to do-do it today-tomorrow may not come. So here goes-As I have told everyone who was so complimentary all my life -ALL the glory belongs to the Lord-not me. I am rotten to the core. I remember Mom telling me when God made me-He threw the mold away because the world could not stand 2 of me. Well, I believe it. I have a big mouth. Bona Griffieth told me I was one of the things they told her to watch out for when she was hired at Roberds, because I would try to get her saved. They did not know she was a Christian and the Lord worked it out she flew home with me when Bobby Joe died. HEY I LOVE that reputation and gladly claim it still today. even on the phone God gives me that boldness.

Bona sent me a sweet note after I returned to FLORIDA to thank me for showing her faith on the plane ride home. Then I got a wonderful letter from Travis Hudson, my Pastor at Moraine Heights Baptist Church. He said after nearly 40 years of preaching-he had never seen faith-until he saw me at Bobby's funeral and thanked me. Clemmon Chappell-one of our preacher boys said I was his Epaphroditus -Rick Glass another GPA preacher-called me our GPA prayer warrior-Bro Dennis Harkins thanked me for being his and his wife's Barnabus. Bro Jim Moore called me a prophetess one morning as he asked I pray for his eye-and the Bro Tolbert Moore at his 90th birthday –was sitting next to a preacher across from me and said he always watched me during the service and if he saw my hand go up he knew the service was okay -if not he wondered what was wrong-because I knew how to get hold of the Holy Spirit. I love you ALL for those kind words.

ALL the glory belongs to Jesus!! I am just so grateful to KNOW why I am on this earth and He enables me to fulfill my commission. He put me here to be a good prayer warrior and an encourager (and He is continually adding to the 3 excel workbooks of names that are called in prayer every Saturday) and of course there is a daily list. Any good you see in me is the LORD. Thanks to ALL of you who allow me to pray for you and encourage you when you are in need. As long as God gives me breath I will continue on this journey of intercessory prayer and encouragement as I spread the Gospel. I will be in Heaven NOT because of what I do but because of what Jesus did at Calvary. Every time we part -my brother Stan says "if I don't see you again over here-I'll see you over there". I say AMEN!!

www.ingramcontent.com/pod-product-compliance
Lightning Source LLC
Chambersburg PA
CBHW031326060726
47590CB00003B/1341